Up
Close
and GROSS
Microscopic Creatures

# ICKY HOUSE INVADERS

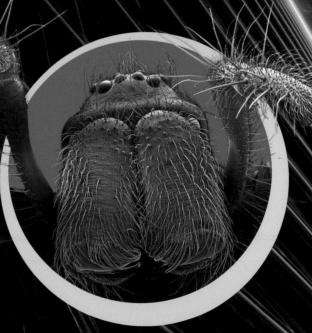

## by Ruth Owen

Consultant: Suzy Gazlay, M.A.
Recipient, Presidential Award
for Excellence in Science Teaching

BEARPORT
PUBLISHING

New York, New York

**Credits**

Cover, © Clouds Hill Imaging/www.lastrefuge.co.uk; CoverBKG, © Paul Prescott/ Shutterstock; 3, © Power and Syred/Science Photo Library; 4, © Clouds Hill Imaging/www.lastrefuge.co.uk; 5, © Clouds Hill Imaging/www.lastrefuge.co.uk; 6, © Nigel Cattlin/FLPA; 7, © Clouds Hill Imaging/www.lastrefuge.co.uk; 8L, © Vita Khorzhevska/Shutterstock; 8R, © Albert Lleal/Minden Pictures/FLPA; 9, © Clouds Hill Imaging/www.lastrefuge.co.uk; 10, © wavebreakmedia ltd/Shutterstock; 11, © Clouds Hill Imaging/www.lastrefuge.co.uk; 12, © Phil McLean/FLPA; 13, © Science Faction/Superstock; 14T, © Nigel Cattlin/FLPA; 14B, © University of Georgia Archive/Bugwood.org; 15, © Clouds Hill Imaging/www.lastrefuge.co.uk; 16, © Nigel Cattlin/FLPA; 17, © Volker Steger/Science Photo Library; 18, © Power and Syred/Science Photo Library; 19, © Robert Harding Picture Library/SuperStock; 20T, © Shutterstock; 20B, © Jack Thomas/Alamy; 21, © Clouds Hill Imaging/www. lastrefuge.co.uk; 22T, © Pascal Goetgheluck/Science Photo Library; 22B, © Scott Bauer/U.S. Department of Agriculture/Science Photo Library.

Publisher: Kenn Goin
Editorial Director: Adam Siegel
Creative Director: Spencer Brinker
Design: Alix Wood
Photo Researcher: Ruby Tuesday Books Ltd


*Library of Congress Cataloging-in-Publication Data*

Owen, Ruth, 1967–
  Icky house invaders / by Ruth Owen.
      p. cm. — (Up close and gross: microscopic creatures)
  Includes bibliographical references and index.
  ISBN-13: 978-1-61772-124-3 (library binding)
  ISBN-10: 1-61772-124-7 (library binding)
  1. Microbiology—Juvenile literature. 2. Household pests—Juvenile literature. I. Title.
  QR57.O945 2011
  616.9'041—dc22

                    2010041241

Published in the United States of America by Bearport Publishing Company, Inc.

For more information, write to Bearport Publishing Company, Inc., 101 Fifth Avenue, Suite 6R, New York, New York 10003. Printed in the United States of America in North Mankato, Minnesota.

121510
10810CGB

10 9 8 7 6 5 4 3 2 1

# Contents

# Who's Living in Your Home?

A house or apartment is not just a place where people and their pets live. It is also a home for thousands of tiny **invaders**. Some of these animals, such as houseflies and spiders, are big enough to see with just your eyes. Others, such as an insect called a book louse, are so small that you need a **microscope** to see them clearly.

In this book you will have a chance to see amazing images of some tiny house invaders. Using powerful microscopes, scientists have zoomed in on these living things to show them up close and in great detail. So get ready to be amazed by the tiny creatures that are sharing your kitchen, carpets, couches—and even your bed!

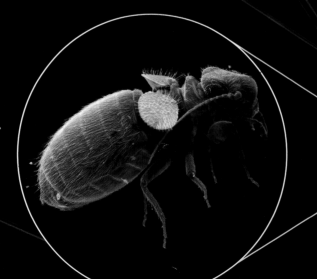

This is the size of real-life book lice.

Book lice live inside old books. They eat paper and the glue that holds books together.

Hairs

In real life, this house spider's body is half an inch (1 cm) long.

The hairs on a spider's body help it find its next meal. How? The hairs can feel **vibrations** that travel through the air when houseflies or other **prey** move nearby.

# Hungry Houseflies

Hungry houseflies are always on the lookout for a meal, so it's not a good idea to leave food uncovered in the kitchen. The problem is that these house invaders don't just eat the food that humans do. They also eat garbage, the dead bodies of animals, and even poop.

When a fly walks on poop or garbage, its feet and body pick up tiny living things called **bacteria**. Then, when the fly walks around on human food, it leaves behind the bacteria. When eaten, some types of bacteria can give humans a very bad upset stomach and **diarrhea**.

Proboscis

A housefly

Houseflies spit special **saliva** onto their food to turn it into a soupy liquid. Then they slurp up the liquid food using a mouthpart called a **proboscis**.

Eye

The housefly's huge eyes allow it to keep watch for enemies in lots of directions.

# Bloodsucking Fleas

Fleas are tiny bloodsucking invaders. They enter houses by hiding in the hair of cats, dogs, and other furry creatures.

Fleas drink blood from animals. To get a meal, a flea pierces an animal's skin using its sharp mouthparts. Then it sucks up the animal's blood. Once it has fed, the flea may stay in carpets, sofas, or pet beds until it needs to drink again. If a flea can't find a furry animal to get blood from, it will jump onto a human for a meal!

Fleas have strong back legs to help them jump up onto an animal or a human.

Back legs

A flea can jump 200 times the length of its body. That's like a person jumping the length of about four football fields!

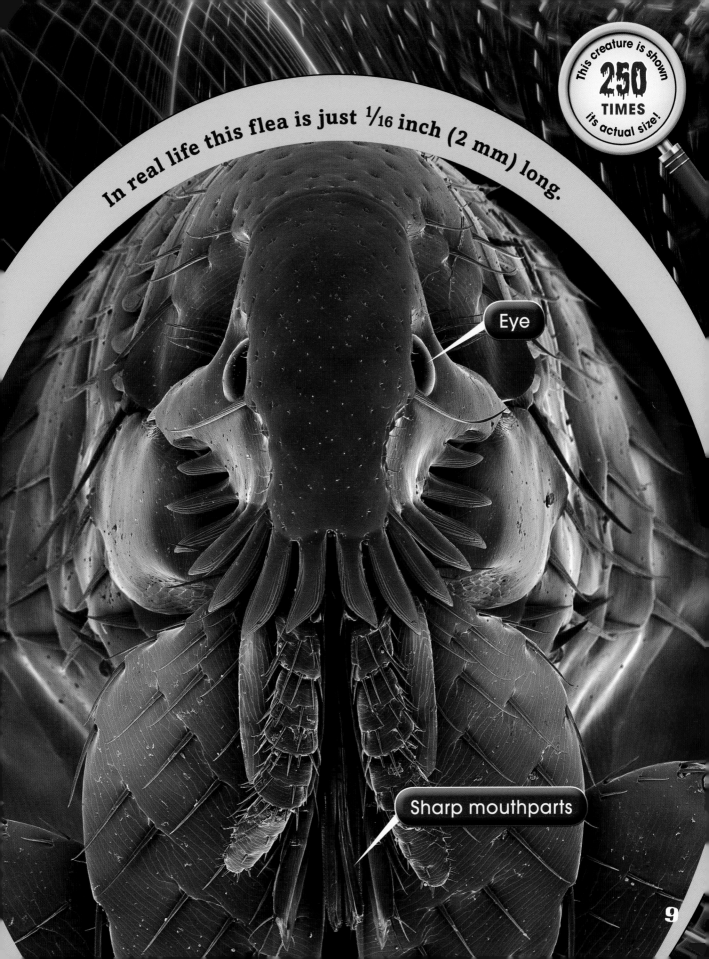

In real life this flea is just ¹/₁₆ inch (2 mm) long.

Eye

Sharp mouthparts

# Dirt-Eating Dust Mites

Every house has some dust in it, but what exactly is dust? Dust is made up of many different ingredients, including dirt, sand, hair, insect poop, and lots of little flakes of skin that fall off people's bodies. There is one tiny house invader that likes to eat these flakes of skin. It is called a dust mite.

Dust mites are eight-legged relatives of spiders. They live in carpets, curtains, sofas, and beds. There can be 100,000 dust mites in one square yard (.8 sq m) of carpet.

It's not possible to see dust mites without a microscope. They are nearly see-through, and their bodies are smaller than the period at the end of this sentence.

An old pillow may be home to thousands of dust mites. It may also contain the bodies of dead dust mites and dust mite poop!

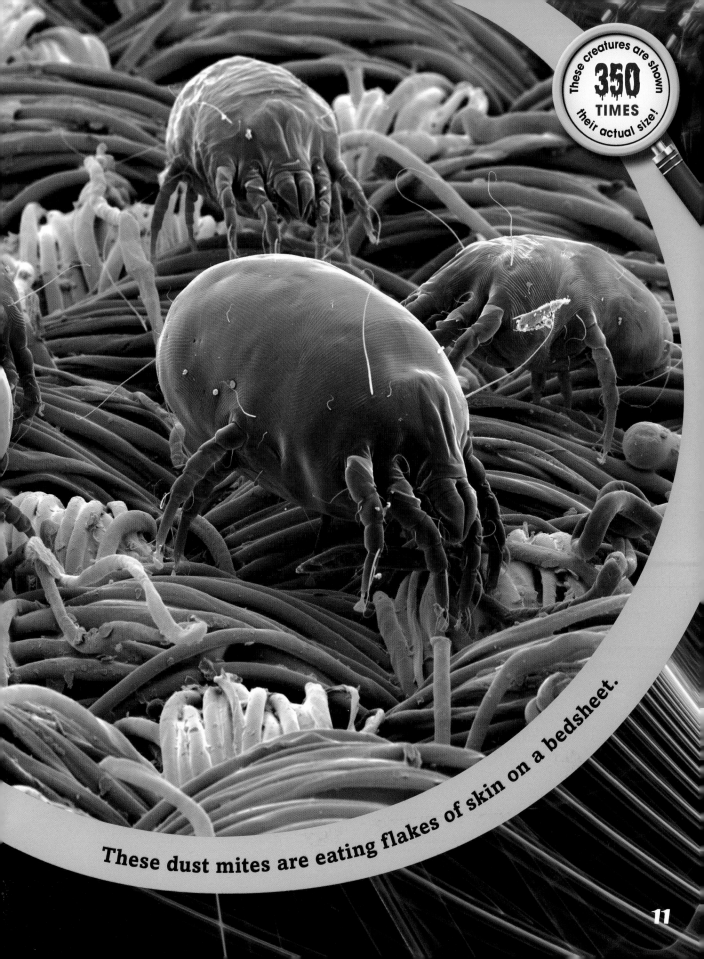

These creatures are shown **350** TIMES their actual size!

These dust mites are eating flakes of skin on a bedsheet.

# Don't Let the Bedbugs Bite!

By day, bedbugs hide under floorboards, behind wallpaper, or in the folds of sheets. By night, these house invaders climb over beds to find human bodies to feed on.

Bedbugs drink human blood. To get it, they pierce a person's skin with their mouthparts and suck! Normally, human blood clots when skin is cut. This means the blood gets thick and sticky so it stops flowing and the cut can heal. Bedbugs, however, have special saliva that stops blood from clotting. As a result, the victim's blood keeps flowing until the bedbug has finished its meal.

Bedbugs sucking blood from a person's arm

Bedbugs can travel in suitcases and clothing, and they are hard to get rid of. Signs of an invasion include tiny spots of dark bedbug poop or little splashes of blood on sheets and other bedding.

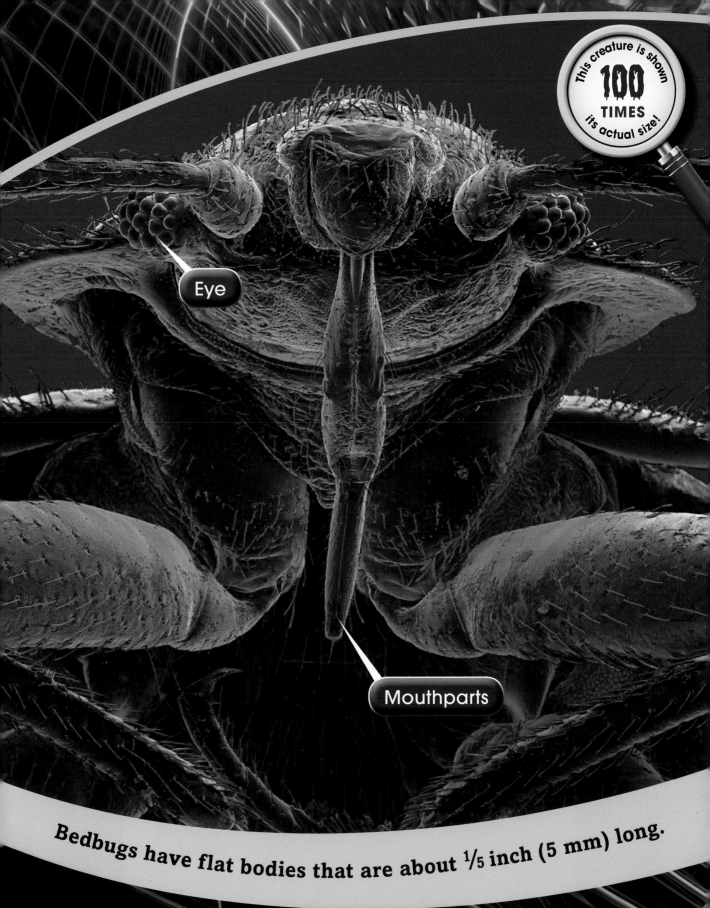

This creature is shown **100** TIMES its actual size!

Eye

Mouthparts

Bedbugs have flat bodies that are about ¹⁄₅ inch (5 mm) long.

# Munching Moths

Clothes moths invade homes so that they can find places to lay their eggs. **Caterpillars** will hatch from the eggs and eventually turn into adult clothes moths.

Moths lay their eggs in places that will give their caterpillars the right food to eat. Unfortunately for people, the right food may be clothes, carpets, curtains, and even teddy bears.

A female moth will lay up to 150 eggs in a dark, safe place. She might choose a shirt hanging in a closet or a sweater stored in an attic. When caterpillars hatch from the eggs, they start munching. By the time the caterpillars have finished eating, the clothing is filled with little holes.

A clothes moth caterpillar

A sweater attacked by clothes moth caterpillars

If you spot moths in a closet, you should wash or dry-clean the clothes to kill the eggs and caterpillars. Placing clothes in the freezer can also help. The cold kills eggs and caterpillars.

Clothes moths are tiny—about $\frac{1}{5}$ inch (5 mm) long.

# Cockroaches in the Kitchen

Cockroaches are a group of insects that often live in people's homes. During the day, they hide in warm, wet places such as basements, drains, and sewers. At night, they come out of their hiding places to find food.

Cockroaches eat almost anything! They feed on garbage, paper, leather, poop, and even one another. They also eat human food, so they head for kitchens to find a meal.

Unfortunately, as they scuttle around kitchen cabinets and countertops they leave behind poop, pee, dirt, and bacteria. The bacteria and filth they leave on food can make humans very ill with diarrhea or food poisoning.

Cockroaches have been around for more than 250 million years. They lived on Earth even before the dinosaurs.

Cockroach poop

This cockroach is just 1/10 inch (2.5 mm) long. It is walking over a plate of cooked carrots.

Head

Antennae

Eggshell

Cockroaches use long body parts called antennae to sniff out food. This cockroach is eating an eggshell.

17

# Furniture-Eating Woodworms

Tiny holes in a wooden chair or table mean wood-eating house invaders have been living in a person's furniture. The woodworm, or furniture beetle, is an insect that lays its eggs on wood. When the beetle's worm-like **larvae**, or young, hatch from the eggs, they **tunnel** into the wood.

Each larva eats its way through the wood, creating longer and longer tunnels. It grows bigger for three to four years. Then the larva becomes a **pupa**. This is the stage during which a larva changes into an adult beetle. The beetle then tunnels out of the wood, leaving behind just a little pile of dust and a telltale hole.

One female furniture beetle can lay around 80 eggs in her lifetime. As a result, the eggs of just two or three female beetles can become a woodworm invasion!

An adult furniture beetle is about 1/10 inch (2.5 mm) long.

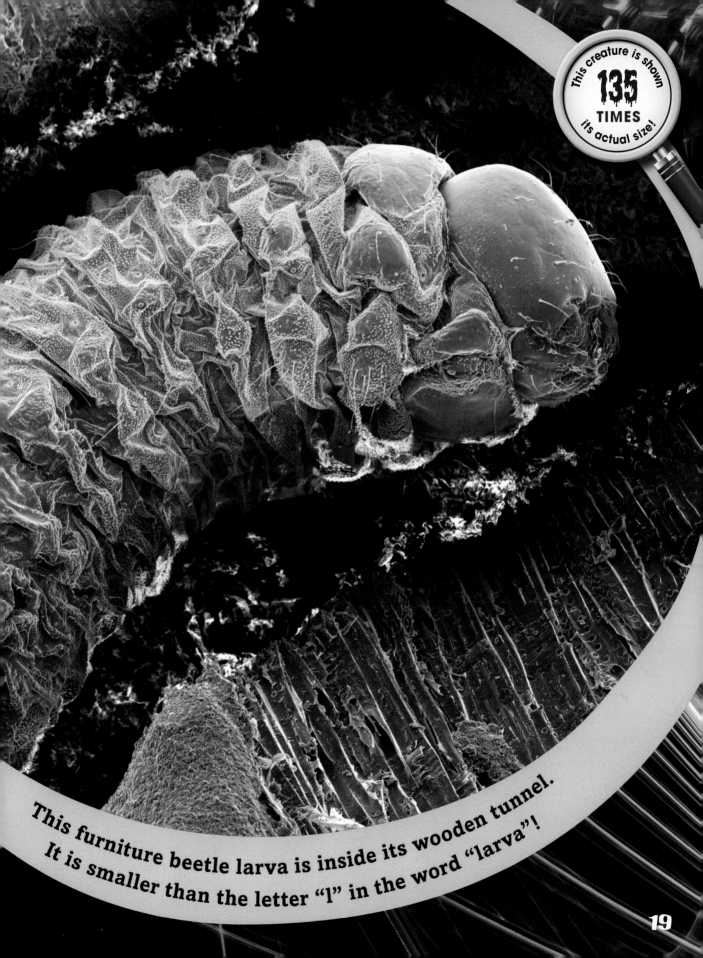

This furniture beetle larva is inside its wooden tunnel.
It is smaller than the letter "l" in the word "larva"!

# Silverfish in Your Sink

The tiny silverfish has been living on Earth for about 300 million years. Scientists have found **fossils** of silverfish that show how the creature's looks have not changed in all that time.

Millions of years ago, silverfish lived in wet areas, such as **swamps**. Today, these insects invade houses and live in bathrooms, sinks, and other cool, **damp** places.

Silverfish come out at night to look for food. They like food that is slightly damp or **starchy**, such as flour, breakfast cereal, sugar, and paper. If a light is switched on, silverfish hurry to the nearest dark place to hide.

The silverfish in this fossil lived about 300 million years ago.

In real life, this modern-day silverfish is half an inch (1 cm) long.

Scales

**Silverfish are covered with tiny scales like those on the skin of fish. That's how silverfish got their name.**

Silverfish have their own roadways to get around in apartment buildings. They use water pipes to travel from apartment to apartment in search of food.

# Getting Up Close

The amazing close-up photographs in this book were created using a very powerful microscope. It is called a scanning **electron** microscope, or SEM.

Microscopes make things look bigger. A scanning electron microscope can show what things look like hundreds of times their real size.

## How were the photos in this book created?

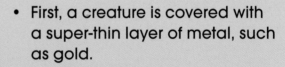

- First, a creature is covered with a super-thin layer of metal, such as gold.

- Next, the SEM passes a beam of tiny particles called electrons over the creature. The electrons bounce off the metal around the creature and create electrical signals. These signals are turned into a black-and-white image of the creature on a computer.

- Scientists then add color to the SEM image using a computer.

# Glossary

**bacteria** (bak-TEER-ee-uh) tiny living things that can only be seen with a microscope; some bacteria are helpful and keep humans and animals healthy; some bacteria are harmful and cause disease

**caterpillars** (KAT-ur-*pil*-urz) the larval, or worm-like, form of young moths and butterflies

**damp** (DAMP) a little wet

**diarrhea** (*dye*-uh-REE-uh) runny, watery body waste that makes a person need to go to the bathroom many times; people and animals may get diarrhea when they have an upset stomach or food poisoning

**electron** (i-LEK-tron) a tiny particle that is found in atoms, the building blocks of all matter; electrons carry electrical charges

**fossils** (FOSS-uhlz) the remains of plants or animals that have turned to rock, or imprints that were made by plants or animals and are preserved in rock

**invaders** (in-VAYD-urz) people or animals that enter a place where they don't normally belong

**larvae** (LAR-vee) the worm-like form of many kinds of young insects; singular form is *larva*

**microscope** (MYE-kruh-skohp) a tool used to see things that are too small to see with the eyes alone

**prey** (PRAY) an animal that is hunted by other animals for food

**proboscis** (pruh-BOS-uhss) a long, tube-like nose or mouthpart used for feeding by some animals, including certain insects such as moths, butterflies, and flies

**pupa** (PYOO-puh) the stage in the life cycle of many insects during which the insect changes from a larva to an adult

**saliva** (suh-LYE-vuh) a clear liquid produced in the mouths of humans and many animals that helps them swallow and chew; also called spit

**starchy** (STAR-chee) having to do with foods containing starch, a white substance that is found in certain plants, such as potatoes, rice, wheat, and corn

**swamps** (SWAHMPS) low areas of land that are mostly flooded and include areas of open water

**tunnel** (TUH-nuhl) to dig or force a passage through something

**vibrations** (vye-BRAY-shuhnz) quick back-and-forth movements that can be felt

# Index

# Bibliography

**Koehler, P. G., and F. M. Oi.** "Fleas." (http://edis.ifas.ufl.edu/ig087)

**Warren, Adrian.** *Unseen Companions: Big Views of Tiny Creatures.* Wells, Somerset, UK: Last Refuge Ltd. (2007).

# Read More

**Llewellyn, Claire.** *The Best Book of Bugs.* New York: Kingfisher (2005).

**Maynard, Christopher.** *Micro Monsters: Life Under the Microscope.* New York: DK Publishing (1999).

**Nguyen, Nam.** *Micro Monsters.* New York: Kingfisher (2010).

# Learn More Online

To learn more about icky house invaders, visit
**www.bearportpublishing.com/UpCloseandGross**

# About the Author

Ruth Owen has been writing children's books for more than ten years. She lives in Cornwall, England, just minutes from the ocean. Ruth loves gardening and caring for her family of llamas.